SY 0012613 6

D1588802

ADC

15,214

ST. MARY'S COLLEGE OF EDUCATION

DATE BORROWED

20/=

Tigers

Fleur Adcock

TIGERS

London
OXFORD UNIVERSITY PRESS
NEW YORK WELLINGTON
1967

15,214

Oxford University Press, Ely House, London W.1

GLASGOW NEW YORK TORONTO MELBOURNE WELLINGTON
CAPE TOWN SALISBURY IBADAN NAIROBI LUSAKA ADDIS ABABA
BOMBAY CALCUTTA MADRAS KARACHI LAHORE DACCA
KUALA LUMPUR HONG KONG TOKYO

© *Oxford University Press 1967*

REFERENCE LIBRARY

ST. MARY'S COLLEGE OF EDUCATION
BELFAST

Section ....*Literature*....

821·91 / ADC

Printed in Great Britain by
The Bowering Press, Plymouth

Contents

Acknowledgements

Acknowledgements are due to the following periodicals in which some of these poems have previously appeared: *Landfall, The Listener, The London Magazine, The New Statesman,* and *The Poetry Book Society's Christmas Pamphlet 1965.*

Acknowledgements are also due to A. H. & A. W. Reed, who published *The Eye of the Hurricane* (Wellington, 1964) in which a number of these poems appeared, and to the B.B.C. Third Programme for poems which have been broadcast in the series 'Poetry Now' and 'The Poet's Voice'.

For a Five-Year-Old

A snail is climbing up the window-sill
Into your room, after a night of rain.
You call me in to see, and I explain
That it would be unkind to leave it there:
It might crawl to the floor; we must take care
That no one squashes it. You understand,
And carry it outside, with careful hand,
To eat a daffodil.

I see, then, that a kind of faith prevails:
Your gentleness is moulded still by words
From me, who have trapped mice and shot wild birds,
From me, who drowned your kittens, who betrayed
Your closest relatives, and who purveyed
The harshest kind of truth to many another.
But that is how things are: I am your mother,
And we are kind to snails.

Miss Hamilton in London

It would not be true to say she was doing nothing:
She visited several bookshops, spent an hour
In the Victoria and Albert Museum (Indian section),
And walked carefully through the streets of Kensington
Carrying five mushrooms in a paper bag,
A tin of black pepper, a literary magazine,
And enough money to pay the rent for two weeks.
The sky was cloudy, leaves lay on the pavements.

Nor did she lack human contacts: she spoke
To three shop-assistants and a newsvendor,
And returned the 'Good-night' of a museum attendant.
Arriving home, she wrote a letter to someone
In Canada, as it might be, or in New Zealand,
Listened to the news as she cooked her meal,
And conversed for five minutes with the landlady.
The air was damp with the mist of late autumn.

A full day, and not unrewarding.
Night fell at the usual seasonal hour.
She drew the curtains, switched on the electric fire,
Washed her hair and read until it was dry,
Then went to bed; where, for the hours of darkness,
She lay pierced by thirty black spears
And felt her limbs numb, her eyes burning,
And dark rust carried along her blood.

Note on Propertius 1.5

Among the Roman love-poets, possession
Is a rare theme. The locked and flower-hung door,
The shivering lover, are allowed. To more
Buoyant moods, the canons of expression
Gave grudging sanction. Do we, then, assume,
Finding Propertius tear-sodden and jealous,
That Cynthia was inexorably callous?
Plenty of moonlight entered that high room
Whose doors had met his Alexandrine battles;
And she, so gay a lutanist, was known
To stitch and doze a night away, alone,
Until the poet tumbled in with apples
For penitence and for her head his wreath,
Brought from a party, of wine-scented roses—
(The garland's aptness lying, one supposes,
Less in the flowers than in the thorns beneath:
Her waking could, he knew, provide his verses
With less idyllic themes.) Onto her bed
He rolled the round fruit, and adorned her head;
Then gently roused her sleeping mouth to curses.
Here the conventions reassert their power:
The apples fall and bruise, the roses wither,
Touched by a sallowed moon. But there were other
Luminous nights—(even the cactus flower
Glows briefly golden, fed by spiny flesh)—
And once, as he acknowledged, all was singing:
The moonlight musical, the darkness clinging,
And she compliant to his every wish.

Hauntings

Three times I have slept in your house
And this is definitely the last.
I cannot endure the transformations:
Nothing stays the same for an hour.

Last time there was a spiral staircase
Winding across the high room.
People tramped up and down it all night,
Carrying brief-cases, pails of milk, bombs,

Pretending not to notice me
As I lay in a bed lousy with dreams.
Couldn't you have kept them away?
After all, they were trespassing.

The time before it was all bathrooms,
Full of naked, quarrelling girls—
And you claim to like solitude:
I do not understand your arrangements.

Now the glass doors to the garden
Open on rows of stone columns;
Beside them stands a golden jeep.
Where are we this time? On what planet?

Every night lasts for a week.
I toss and turn and wander about,
Whirring from room to room like a moth,
Ignored by those indifferent faces.

At last I think I have woken up.
I lift my head from the pillow, rejoicing.
The alarm-clock is playing Schubert:
I am still asleep. This is too much.

Well, I shall try again in a minute.
I shall wake into this real room
With its shadowy plants and patterned screens
(Yes, I remember how it looks.)

It will be cool, but I shan't wait
To light the gas-fire. I shall dress
(I know where my clothes are) and slip out.
You needn't think I am here to stay.

Night-Piece

1 *Beginning*

I am afraid of your deep world.
And yet I turn to you, from those
With whom I swung on cadences of sunshine;
Those whose flesh was fruit to my mouth, whose skin
Smooth as apple-rind and their eyes golden;
Who tasted of wine and honey.

Now I move on a different axis.
With you I gaze through the close channel
Of a telescope at half-predictable stars;
Talking together, we trace their cogent circles,
And making love, we sink down through a dark
Well, into sweet water.

2 *Before Sleep*

Lying close to your heart-beat, my lips
Touching the pulse in your neck, my head on your arm,
I listen to your hidden blood as it slips
With a small furry sound along the warm
Veins; and my slowly-flowering dream
Of Chinese landscapes, river-banks and flying
Splits into sudden shapes—children who scream
By a roadside, blinded men, a woman lying
In a bed filled with blood: the broken ones.
We are so vulnerable. I curl towards
That intricate machine of nerves and bones
With its built-in life: your body. And to your words
I whisper 'Yes' and 'Always', as I lie
Waiting for thunder from a stony sky.

3 *Dreaming*

Backwards through many modes of being
We have moved into this cool sea-current

Where in undifferentiated form
We are the grey-green tide that we inhabit.
At first high in a rocky landscape
We watched or were archaic heroes,
Tangled in myth and brittle with tradition,
Who followed out the patterns of a quest;
And meeting for the scene of conflict
Found all transformed by rippling light.
Then the pulsating union of great cats,
Furred and fierce, with grey eyes—our eyes.
The air shifted and grew still;
Surf rose from a slow sea,
And plants, set like fleshy stars in the rocks,
Read without eyes each other's history.
So the protean pictures passed
And fell away. Now we are water,
Or almost water—plankton or protozoa,
Adrift in a distant wash of sucking tides.
Still our mythology clings about us;
Still we meet, and still combine.

4 Waking

My eyes open with a click
And meet your eyes, fixed on mine
With a steady gaze that licks at my waking face
Patiently, like a gentle tongue, and clinging
As fur to fingers. Even when I blink
I can hear you watching me.

Daylight shouting at the windows
Recalls the sky of sun-shot cloud,
The world of times and weather. To which we turn
Without reluctance, now. There is no need
For your hand on my breast or your light breath in my hair:
Your silent gaze holds me.

Incident

When you were lying on the white sand,
A rock under your head, and smiling,
(Circled by dead shells), I came to you
And you said, reaching to take my hand,
'Lie down'. So for a time we lay
Warm on the sand, talking and smoking,
Easy; while the grovelling sea behind
Sucked at the rocks and measured the day.
Lightly I fell asleep then, and fell
Into a cavernous dream of falling.
It was all the cave-myths, it was all
The myths of tunnel or tower or well—
Alice's rabbit-hole into the ground,
Or the path of Orpheus: a spiral staircase
To hell, furnished with danger and doubt.
Stumbling, I suddenly woke; and found
Water about me. My hair was wet,
And you were sitting on the grey sand,
Waiting for the lapping tide to take me:
Watching, and lighting a cigarette.

Instructions to Vampires

I would not have you drain
With your sodden lips the flesh that has fed mine,
And leech his bubbling blood to a decline:
Not that pain;

Nor visit on his mind
That other desiccation, where the wit
Shrivels: so to be humbled is not fit
For his kind.

But use acid or flame,
Secretly, to brand or cauterize;
And on the soft globes of his mortal eyes
Etch my name.

The Eye of the Hurricane

Ringed about with black fire
We see the lightning crackle in our vineyards.

The burnt and smoking air rises
Dark with wine-fumes in a dead spiral,

And to our left the sea boils
Inward in spastic waves. Only above

The sky is held in a tight bowl
Of rigid calm. Here, once, in a different quietness,

Careless with fishing-boats and warm
With a milky breeze, we walked the waves' edge,

Swam naked in the rollicking sea,
And lay on the sand eating cool grapes

Smooth to the sucking tongue, their seeds
Gritty as we crunched them with laughing teeth.

There were dragons then, salamanders
Trickling among the rocks; and the lemon-tree flowered.

How long is it since we saw
The horizon churning about us in a vortex,

How long since we were trapped in stillness?
Our crops are smouldering now on the grey slopes,

The air thickens with ash. Soon,
As we look towards each other in sick desire

(Eyes blank to kinder feelings,)
The impatient wind will turn inwards and choke us.

Parting is such sweet Sorrow

The room is full of clichés—'Throw me a crumb'
And 'Now I see the writing on the wall'
And, 'Don't take umbrage, dear.' I wish I could.
Instead I stand bedazzled by them all,

Longing for shade. Belshazzar's fiery script
Glows there, between the prints of tropical birds,
In neon lighting, and the air is full
Of crumbs that flash and click about me. Words

Glitter in colours like those gaudy prints:
The speech of a computer, metal-based
But feathered like a cloud of darts. All right.
Your signal-system need not go to waste.

Mint me another batch of tokens: say
'I am in your hands; I throw myself upon
Your mercy, casting caution to the winds.'
Thank you; there is no need to go on.

Thus authorized by your mechanical
Issue, I lift you like a bale of hay,
Open the window wide, and toss you out;
And gales of laughter whirl you far away.

Unexpected Visit

I have nothing to say about this garden.
I do not want to be here, I can't explain
What happened. I merely opened a usual door
And found this. The rain

Has just stopped, and the gravel paths are trickling
With water. Stone lions, on each side,
Gleam like wet seals, and the green birds
Are stiff with dripping pride.

Not my kind of country. The gracious vistas,
The rose-gardens and terraces, are all wrong—
As comfortless as the weather. But here I am.
I cannot tell how long

I have stood gazing at grass too wet to sit on,
Under a sky so dull I cannot read
The sundial, staring along the curving walks
And wondering where they lead;

Not really hoping, though, to be enlightened.
It must be morning, I think, but there is no
Horizon behind the trees, no sun as clock
Or compass. I shall go

And find, somewhere among the formal hedges
Or hidden behind a trellis, a toolshed. There
I can sit on a box and wait. Whatever happens
May happen anywhere.

And better, perhaps, among the rakes and flowerpots
And sacks of bulbs than under this pallid sky:
Having chosen nothing else, I can at least
Choose to be warm and dry.

The Man who X-rayed an Orange

Viewed from the top, he said, it was like a wheel,
The paper-thin spokes raying out from the hub
To the half-transparent circumference of rind,
With small dark ellipses suspended between.
He could see the wood of the table-top through it.
Then he knelt, and with his eye at orange-level
Saw it as the globe, its pithy core
Upright from pole to flattened pole. Next,
Its levitation: sustained (or so he told us)
By a week's diet of nothing but rice-water
He had developed powers, drawing upon which
He raised it to a height of about two feet
Above the table, with never a finger near it.
That was all. It descended, gradually opaque,
To rest; while he sat giddy and shivering.
(He shivered telling it.) But surely, we asked,
(And still none of us mentioned self-hypnosis
Or hallucinations caused by lack of food,)
Surely triumphant too? Not quite, he said,
With his little crooked smile. It was not enough:
He should have been able to summon up,
Created out of what he had newly learnt,
A perfectly imaginary orange, complete
In every detail; whereupon the real orange
Would have vanished. Then came explanations
And his talk of mysticism, occult physics,
Alchemy, the Qabalah—all his hobby-horses.
If there was failure, it was only here
In the talking. For surely he had lacked nothing,
Neither power nor insight nor imagination,
When he knelt alone in his room, seeing before him
Suspended in the air that golden globe,
Visible and transparent, light-filled:
His only fruit from the Tree of Life.

Flight, with Mountains

(In Memory of David Herron)

Tarmac, take-off: metallic words conduct us
Over that substance, black with spilt rain,
To this event. Sealed, we turn and pause.
Engines churn and throb to a climax, then
Up: a hard spurt, and the passionate rise
Levels out for this gradual incline.

There was something of pleasure in that thrust
From earth into ignorant cloud; but here,
Above all tremors of sensation, rest
Replaces motion; secretly we enter
The obscurely gliding current, and encased
In vitreous calm inhabit the high air.

Now I see, beneath the plated wing,
Cloud edges withdrawing their slow foam
From shoreline, rippling hills, and beyond, the long
Crested range of the land's height. I am
Carried too far by this blind rocketing:
Faced with mountains, I remember him

Whose death seems a convention of such a view:
Another one for the mountains. Another one
Who, climbing to stain the high snow
With his shadow, fell, and briefly caught between
Sudden earth and sun, projected below
A flicker of darkness; as, now, this plane.

2

Only air to hold the wings;
Only words to hold the story;
Only a frail web of cells
To hold heat in the body.

14

Breath bleeds from throat and lungs
Under the last cold fury;
Words wither; meaning fails;
Steel wings grow heavy.

3

Headlines announced it, over a double column of type:
The cabled facts, public regret, and a classified list
Of your attainments—degrees, scholarships and positions,
And notable feats of climbing. So the record stands:
No place there for my private annotations. The face
That smiles in some doubt from a fuscous half-tone block
Stirs me hardly more than those I have mistaken
Daily, about the streets, for yours.
                                        I can refer
To my own pictures; and turning first to the easiest,
Least painful, I see Dave the raconteur,
Playing a shoal of listeners on a casual line
Of dry narration. Other images unreel:
Your face in a car, silent, watching the dark road,
Or animated and sunburnt from your hard pleasures
Of snow and rock-face; again, I see you arguing,
Practical and determined, as you draw with awkward puffs
At a rare cigarette.
                        So much, in vivid sequence
Memory gives. And then, before I can turn away,
Imagination adds the last scene: your eyes bruised,
Mouth choked under a murderous weight of snow.

4

'When you reach the top of a mountain, keep on climbing'—
Meaning, we may suppose,
To sketch on space the cool arabesques of birds
In plastic air, or those
Exfoliating arcs, upward and outward,
Of an aeronautic show.
Easier, such a free fall in reverse,

Higher than clogging snow
Or clutching gravity, than the awkward local
Embrace of rocks. And observe
The planets coursing their elliptical race-tracks,
Where each completed curve
Cinctures a new dimension. Mark these patterns.
Mark, too, how the high
Air thins. The top of any mountain
Is a base for the sky.

5

Further by days and oceans than all my flying
You have gone, while here the air insensibly flowing
Over a map of mountains drowns my dumbness.
A turn of the earth away, where a crawling dimness
Waits now to absorb our light, another
Snowscape, named like this one, took you; and neither
Rope, nor crumbling ice, nor your unbelieving
Uncommitted hands could hold you to living.
Wheels turn; the dissolving air rolls over
An arc of thunder. Gone is gone forever.

For Andrew

'Will I die?' you ask. And so I enter on
The dutiful exposition of that which you
Would rather not know, and I rather not tell you.
To soften my 'Yes' I offer compensations—
Age and fulfilment ('It's so far away;
You will have children and grandchildren by then')
And indifference ('By then you will not care').
No need: you cannot believe me, convinced
That if you always eat plenty of vegetables
And are careful crossing the street you will live for ever.
And so we close the subject, with much unsaid—
This, for instance: Though you and I may die
Tomorrow or next year, and nothing remain
Of our stock, of the unique, preciously-hoarded
Inimitable genes we carry in us,
It is possible that for many generations
There will exist, sprung from whatever seeds,
Children straight-limbed, with clear enquiring voices,
Bright-eyed as you. Or so I like to think:
Sharing in this your childish optimism.

The Lover

Always he would inhabit an alien landscape,
Someone else's setting; he walked with surly
Devotion the moist paths of a bush valley
Whose trees had spoken to one he could not keep
As friend; he would learn local names, claim kinship
By an act of will; then let his mind haunt
And cling as hands grasped branches, stones,
Eyes learnt by heart another sky's shape.

In late childhood he had lived a year
Emotionally wedded to an elm, whose leaves
Crumbling in all his pockets evoked rough
And bitter the warm bark; then a small creek
Had filled one summer with the breathing air
Of willows and brown water; by such loving
He cast off abounding, more exacting dreams,
And baffled others less than he would think.

Later, his enlarging world demanded
Mountains, passionate rivers, a harsh bay,
As wider symbols; where no loved face
Spread to his hand, he would stroke wind-grained wood,
Learn and cherish a stone's contours, and,
Where once the grace of a girl's voice had spoken,
Set blind feet on the hare's path to walk
And closet with a rock his loving blood.

The climax never came; he might have cooled
His flesh utterly in the sudden river,
Or found long satisfaction in a haven
Made solitary by hills; but gradually
The challenging lust ebbed back unfulfilled.
Now, set apart, he lets the city's plan
Absorb him calmly; only now and then
Stares at the harbour, at the vivid sea.

After the Board-Meeting

He walks through the gardens, lopping the heads
Off tulips with his umbrella. Today's meeting
Did not go well. A trail of slaughtered petals
Follows him along the flowerbeds.

He needs a drink. He knows he has smoked too much.
The hairs in his nostrils itch with nicotine.
Frustration churns in his guts. He should have handled
Those people better. Is he losing his touch?

Over to his left, the river is grey.
Glass towers fringe it, and bevelled cubes
Built in the thirties but not, to him, quaint.
His period. He slashes memories away.

O tempora, o flumen, o river of—what?
Of time, he must suppose. He is forty-nine,
Looks sixty. There was the war, of course:
An excuse, could he accept it; he does not.

He is what he has become. Now, with brisk tread,
He stalks past the shrubbery, glares at children,
And turns his eyes away from lovers. Anger,
His chief passion, glows from his bald head.

How to escape the long cause of this rage?
Possibilities march into his mind—
Drugs, religion, suicide, some trick
To erase the records, to open a new page.

What about madness, now? That might be best.
He could strip off his clothes, leap into the fountain,
Splash water at the lovers, float his hat
Across the pool, and when he wanted to rest

Adopt a foetal posture on the lawn
And await the inevitably-summoned van,
The white room, the nurses, the injections,
The sleep that would last, for once, until dawn.

But no: there are imperfections in the plan.
Ill-informed though he is about madness,
He knows that it is not oblivion.
And anyway, such conduct in a man

In his position will not do. The board
Might appoint that uncouth Jenkins in his place;
And think of the effect on the committee!
It is all more of a risk than he can afford.

A few stiff drinks instead, then. On he goes,
Stabbing the gravel paths with his umbrella,
Towards whisky and his luncheon at the club—
Mad enough, and madder than he knows.

The House

I have been all around the house
And there is nothing, no one. I
Was the only figure you saw
Walking in the garden. I found
A dead magpie and a live cat:
That was all. They were both silent.
I even climbed a ladder, right
Up on to the roof, and found it
Empty. Did you think there would be
Rooks, bursting from the chimney-pots,
Scattering soot and wild noise? No,
There was nothing. Inside the house
I searched every room, opened
Cupboard doors, listened at windows.
Nothing rattled—there is no wind
Tonight—and the stairs did not creak.
In the attic I heard only
My own sounds—the breath whispering
In my throat, and the dull beating,
Inside my ears, of my own pulse.

So you see it is all quite safe.
You can come back—come tomorrow,
Perhaps, in daylight. We could sit
By the fire; we could drink white wine,
Eat chicken sandwiches for lunch,
Listen to records. Please come back.
I can't stay in this house alone.

ST. MARY'S COLLEGE OF EDUCATION
FALLS ROAD, BELFAST, 12.

Advice to a Discarded Lover

Think, now: if you have found a dead bird,
Not only dead, not only fallen,
But full of maggots: what do you feel—
More pity or more revulsion?

Pity is for the moment of death,
And the moments after. It changes
When decay comes, with the creeping stench
And the wriggling, munching scavengers.

Returning later, though, you will see
A shape of clean bone, a few feathers,
An inoffensive symbol of what
Once lived. Nothing to make you shudder.

It is clear. then, But perhaps you find
The analogy I have chosen
For our dead affair rather gruesome—
Too unpleasant a comparison.

It is not accidental. In you
I see maggots close to the surface.
You are eaten up by self-pity,
Crawling with unlovable pathos.

If I were to touch you I should feel
Against my fingers fat, moist worm-skin.
Do not ask me for charity now:
Go away until your bones are clean.

Regression

All the flowers have gone back into the ground.
We fell on them, and they did not lie
Crushed and crumpled, waiting to die
On the earth's surface. No: they suddenly wound

The film of their growth backwards. We saw them shrink
From blossom to bud to tiny shoot,
Down from the stem and up from the root.
Back to the seed, brothers. It makes you think.

Clearly they do not like us. They've gone away,
Given up. And who could blame
Anything else for doing the same?
I notice that certain trees look smaller today.

You can't escape the fact: there's a backward trend
From oak to acorn, and from pine
To cone; they all want to resign.
Understandable enough, but where does it end?

Harder, you'd think, for animals; yet the cat
Was pregnant, but has not produced.
Her rounded belly is reduced,
Somehow, to normal. How to answer that?

Buildings, perhaps, will be the next to go;
Imagine it: a tinkle of glass,
A crunch of brick, and a house will pass
Through the soil to the protest meeting below.

This whole conspiracy of inverted birth
Leaves only us; and how shall we
Endure as we deserve to be,
Foolish and lost on the naked skin of the earth?

Composition for Words and Paint

This darkness has a quality
That poses us in shapes and textures,
One plane behind another,
Flatness in depth.

Your face; a fur of hair; a striped
Curtain behind, and to one side cushions;
Nothing recedes, all lies extended.
I sink upon your image.

I see a soft metallic glint,
A tinsel weave behind the canvas,
Aluminium and bronze beneath the ochre.
There is more in this than we know.

I can imagine drawn around you
A white line, in delicate brush-strokes:
Emphasis; but you do not need it.
You have completeness.

I am not measuring your gestures;
(I have seen you measure those of others,
Know a mind by a hand's trajectory,
The curve of a lip.)

But you move, and I move towards you,
Draw back your head, and I advance.
I am fixed to the focus of your eyes.
I share your orbit.

Now I discover things about you:
Your thin wrists, a tooth missing;
And how I melt and burn before you.
I have known you always.

The greyness from the long windows
Reduces visual depth; but tactile
Reality defies half-darkness.
My hands prove you solid.

You draw me down upon your body,
Hard arms behind my head.
Darkness and soft colours blur.
We have swallowed the light.

Now I dissolve you in my mouth,
Catch in the corners of my throat
The sly taste of your love, sliding
Into me, singing.

Just as the birds have started singing.
Let them come flying through the windows
With chains of opals around their necks.
We are expecting them.

The Water Below

This house is floored with water,
Wall to wall, a deep green pit,
Still and gleaming, edged with stone.
Over it are built stairways
And railed living-areas
In wrought iron. All rather
Impractical; it will be
Damp in winter, and we shall
Surely drop small objects—keys,
Teaspoons, or coins—through the chinks
In the ironwork, to splash
Lost into the glimmering
Depths (and do we know how deep?)
It will have to be rebuilt:
A solid floor of concrete
Over this dark well (perhaps
Already full of coins, like
The flooded crypt of that church
In Ravenna.) You might say
It could be drained, made into
A useful cellar for coal.
But I am sure the water
Would return; would never go.
Under my grandmother's house
In Drury, when I was three,
I always believed there was
Water: lift up the floorboards
And you would see it—a lake,
A subterranean sea.
True, I played under the house
And saw only hard-packed earth,
Wooden piles, gardening tools,
A place to hunt for lizards.
That was different: below
I saw no water. Above,
I knew it must still be there,

Waiting. (For why did we say
'Forgive us our trespasses,
Deliver us from evil?')
Always beneath the safe house
Lies the pool, the hidden sea
Created before we were.
It is not easy to drain
The waters under the earth.

Remarks on Sernyl

The drug required of me, it seemed, the rehearsal
Of a static, sunny, twenty-year-old moment
When a caterpillar crawled onto my sandal,
(I a child in a cornfield.) Its sinuous movement
And silky stripes—purple or black or brown
On dazzling yellow—must be recreated
In words; and I pursued the image down
Tunnels of light-waves. Unseen thousands waited.
Here, then, compounded of these elements—
The bright, vibrant obsession, the sensation
Of an urgent and receptive audience—
Was madness, brief and factitious: the creation
Of a chemical imbalance, such as may
Twist any mental eye asquint, or make
The deaf hear demons. Hitler had, they say,
A sugar deficiency, and craved sweet cake;
And who knows what disordered blood flowed through
Caligula's veins, or drummed in Xerxes' head
When he caused the sea to be whipped? All we need do
Is to put all our warmongers to bed
And inject, to reverse the balance, a milder folly.
Then let us see them relax from ranting gestures
And shunt themselves off, each on his docile trolley,
Into a pink Nirvana of shapes and textures.

The Cave

I used to be puzzled
At her obsession with furniture—
Gas-stoves, kettles, curtains,
Tables and chairs. Now it is clearer.
Waking in the mornings
With her cold question, she could glance at
The room and see the same
Leaf-patterned curtains, the mirror still
Reflecting the lampshade;
And know herself still the same (touching
Her hair, in case it had
Grown in the night, and twitching her toes
To estimate her height.)

For myself, I have chosen a cave.
It has no furniture
Except what I could hardly avoid—
Boxes to store my books,
A stool and table which I have made,
A pot to boil my soup,
A mattress (bracken does not grow here,
And straw would make me sneeze.)
My days are regular, undisturbed.

I wake in the mornings
And see, if I have left the entrance
Uncovered, spider-webs
Stretched across the cave-mouth, strung with dew.
(How would she feel about
Spider-webs, I wonder—their patterns
Different each morning:
Or, for that matter, about a cave?)

I go to fetch water
From the spring, collect and chop firewood
(There is a stone on which

I keep my axe sharp), tend the garden
(Herbs and vegetables:
Beans grow well here, and little turnips.)
Sometimes I find mushrooms
Or nuts, and every week I go
To the farm for eggs, cheese,
Salt and oatmeal. Often they give me
Olives and figs as well.
It is half a day's journey from here.
(I sometimes think of her
Shopping in the supermarket, fixed
Nervously by a shelf
Of tins, hesitating between three
Brands of coffee, in four
Different sizes.)

                    To light my fire
I have a tinder-box
(Home-made), and I use a bunch of twigs
For sweeping the stone floor.
(She uses a vacuum-cleaner,
Emptying out the dust
Afterwards on to a newspaper
Where she can carefully
Pick out any paper-clips or pins.)

I spend the afternoons
Reading; I have read all of Virgil,
And made some translations
From the Georgics. Or I go and walk
In the woods, to find plants
And insects, and make notes and drawings
Of them. As for writing,
That seems not to come as easily
As I had hoped. I sit
At the cave's entrance, and stare across
The valley, in the full
Light. (Not like her, twirling
The ribbon of her typewriter back

And forth as she struggles
To frame a sentence, refusing to
Look out of the window.)
I see all the colours of the day
Spread out for my vision.
But there is nothing I need to write:
Not even a letter
(I know no one) or a diary
(My days are all the same.)
I am here. It has to be enough
Just to be so much here.

I Ride on my High Bicycle

I ride on my high bicycle
Into a sooty Victorian city
Of colonnaded bank buildings,
Horse-troughs, and green marble fountains.

I glide along, contemplating
The curly lettering on the shop-fronts.
An ebony elephant, ten feet tall,
Is wheeled past, advertising something.

When I reach the dark archway
I chain my bicycle to a railing,
Nod to a policeman, climb the steps,
And emerge into unexpected sunshine.

There below lies Caroline Bay,
Its red roofs and its dazzling water.
Now I am running along the path;
It is four o'clock, there is still just time.

I halt and sit on the sandy grass
To remove my shoes and thick stockings;
But something has caught me; around my shoulders
I feel barbed wire; I am entangled.

It pulls my hair, dragging me downwards;
I am suddenly older than seventeen,
Tired, powerless, pessimistic.
I struggle weakly; and wake, of course.

Well, all right. It doesn't matter.
Perhaps I didn't get to the beach:
But I have been there—to all the beaches,
(Waking or dreaming), and all the cities.

Now it is very early morning
And from my window I see a leopard
Tall as a horse, majestic and kindly,
Padding over the fallen snow.

Think before you Shoot

Look, children, the wood is full of tigers,
Scorching the bluebells with their breath.
You reach for guns. Will you preserve the flowers
At such cost? Will you prefer the death
Of prowling stripes to a mush of trampled stalks?
Through the eyes, then—do not spoil the head.
Tigers are easier to shoot than to like.
Sweet necrophiles, you only love them dead.

There now, you've got three—and with such fur, too,
Golden and warm and salty. Very good.
Don't expect them to forgive you, though.
There are plenty more of them. This is their wood
(And their bluebells, which you have now forgotten.)
They've eaten all the squirrels. They want you,
And it's no excuse to say you're only children.
No one is on your side. What will you do?

Tigers

I try not to write about tigers,
But when I try to write about us
On they come, their smooth coats rippling with
Light, their eyes fixed on the horizon.
They do not look at us; they do not
Greet us as their cousins. Why should we
Imagine that we resemble them?

We do not, in fact, fight like tigers.
Look, the cubs are only playing: you
Would think their teeth made of rubber, and
Their pretty claws. We hurt. We draw blood.
The grown ones, too, do not fight. We may
See them gliding out softly, at night,
Together. They are going to kill
Something else: not to hurt each other.
Why should they tear gold and black striped fur,
Gulp tigers' blood? They have other prey.
We must admire their common sense.

                                    This
Is the first lesson from the tigers.
Then there is the lesson of patience,
And the lesson of watchfulness. Look
At their eyes—golden, unblinking, sure.
Our eyes are grey, with a tawny ring
Around the pupil, like a circle
Of fur: identical, yours with mine.
(We think we understand what this means:
We are too alike, we say.) Tigers
Do not use their eyes on each other
As weapons—nor in these long sucking
Glances, that hold us together, drained
Of breath. Tigers are above such things.

35

These tigers will have to go. They are
A distraction. There is one thing, though,
That I should like to tell them: Listen,
Tigers, I would say: you think you know
All you need—burning, as the man said,
In your forests; but we could teach you.
They would listen remotely, as I
Tried to describe for them a matter
In which we approach them: there is a
Felinity in our best actions.
But what else there is in our loving
They cannot know, nor can I tell them.
Let them go, then, uncomprehending.
If they could understand even they,
The proud tigers, might be envious.

The Pangolin

There have been all those tigers, of course,
And a leopard, and a six-legged giraffe,
And a young deer that ran up to my window
Before it was killed, and once a blue horse,
And somewhere an impression of massive dogs.
Why do I dream of such large, hot-blooded beasts
Covered with sweating fur and full of passions
When there could be dry lizards and cool frogs,
Or slow, modest creatures, as a rest
From all those panting, people-sized animals?
Hedgehogs or perhaps tortoises would do,
But I think the pangolin would suit me best:
A vegetable animal, who goes
Disguised as an artichoke or asparagus-tip
In a green coat of close-fitting leaves,
With his flat shovel-tail and his pencil-nose:
The scaly anteater. Yes, he would fit
More aptly into a dream than into his cage
In the Small Mammal House; so I invite him
To be dreamt about, if he would care for it.